A SLEEPOVER WITH STRETCH

Don't forget your paw jamas ☺

Written and Illustrated
by Justin Beaton

The book is dedicated to all the
little dreamers in the world. May
the Lord's plans give you a
future and a hope.

A special thanks goes to Amy Beaton for proofreading
and editing this book and to Milani, Leo, and Mateo for
sleeping over and having so much fun with us.

STRETCH

Good morning, Stretch! Are you excited about your cousins coming over for the **big sleepover?**

"Meow! Of course, I am! But first, I have to use Amy's makeup mirror to make sure I look my very best when they arrive!"

It's time for Justin to set up the tent fort and the air mattress. This sleepover is going to be so much fun.

Look at the name on the air mattress!

Stretch's cousins, Milani, Leo, and Mateo, arrive and it's time for the sleepover to start!

The kids just came inside, and Stretch is already playing hide-and-seek.

He found a good spot under the table, but the boys found him!

Look! Stretch and Milani are by the window. Milani is good at taking care of Stretch. Milani and Leo also like to play kitties, but wait, where did they get those crazy cat shirts?

Milani wrote a silly to-do list for the
sleepover. It looks like we're having
pretzel chicken for dinner and making
blue whale sounds.

Raise your hand if you can sound
like a blue whale!

The sleepover tent is almost complete. If everyone helps, we will **finish in no time.**

There's always time for an ice cream break.

Back inside, it's time to brush our teeth and get ready for the movie!

All of God's critters big and small are getting ready for bed, but at the sleepover with Stretch, the movie is just getting started.

There he is! Stretch is getting cozy for the movie too.

Everyone is watching. This must
be a good part!

Hey, Stretch, don't fall asleep yet. The movie is just starting to get good.

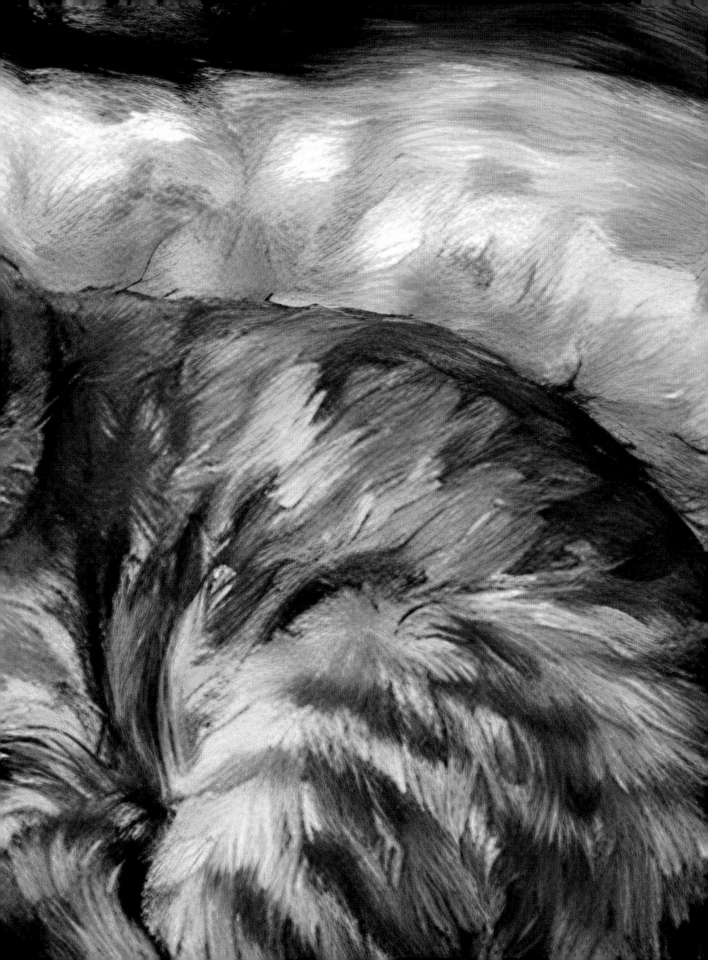

Watching that movie together under the sleepover tent was so much fun, but now it's bedtime.

Before we go to sleep, we must pray and thank God for a fun sleepover and the promise of more adventures tomorrow.

The whole town is in their beds dreaming,
and the sleepover cousins are going to sleep
too.
Sleep tight because tomorrow we will be
going somewhere **really neat!**

Hooray, Leo! It's morning!

What should we make for
breakfast before we go on
our special trip?

Stretch, you're supposed to
be downstairs helping us
make breakfast...

Waffles and sausage. **YUM!** Who's excited about the big adventure today?

Leo is brushing his teeth after breakfast and watching morning cartoons while Milani feeds Stretch.

The girls change and put makeup on to get ready. I can't wait to see this **very special place!**

CRAZY

Before we go, we should clean up everything from the sleepover, but it looks like it's getting a little crazy!

It's time to go!

We don't want
to be late.

Justin, Amy, Milani, Leo, and Mateo, head out together to drive to the special place.

The kids still don't know where it is, but they will find out soon...

Surprise! It's the **Milwaukee Museum.** But wait, the coolest part is still to come...

Stretch couldn't come to the museum
because he has a lot of cat-napping to do
back home.

He must be tired from all the sleepover fun.

It's time for the best part of today's trip. It's a movie about **blue whales** on the **gigantic screen!**

Wow, look how big that blue whale is all the way up there on the **giant movie screen!**

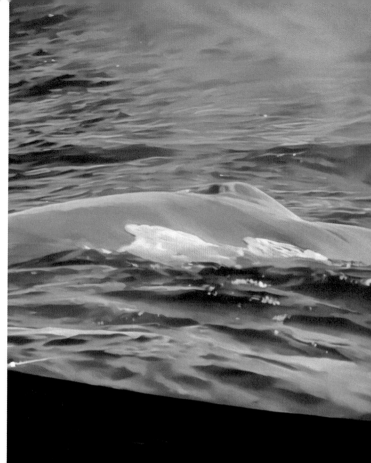

I think the boys wish that they could jump into the ocean and go swimming with the blue whales.

We are all using our imaginations today, and it is **so much fun**.

Look at that! The kids look so tiny compared to the blue whale tail. That's pretty neat, don't you think?

LUNCH

After an exciting day, Stretch's cousins are hungry. Time for lunch!

Our special trip has come to an end, and it's time to take the cousins back to their house. Oh, look at that! It's a cute duck family crossing the street. I wonder if these ducks have ever seen a mighty blue whale?

His cousins are back at their house tonight, and Stretch misses them very much. He had **so much fun** at the sleepover, but he forgot to bring out his special light machine that puts stars on the ceiling!

I guess he will have to show them at the next sleepover. Goodnight, Stretch! We hope your dreams are **stretchy and furry.**

Meet Author Justin Beaton

Justin and his lovely wife, Amy, live in Wisconsin with the stretchiest feline that you ever did see. They are starting their family and can't wait to introduce their future kids to Stretch!

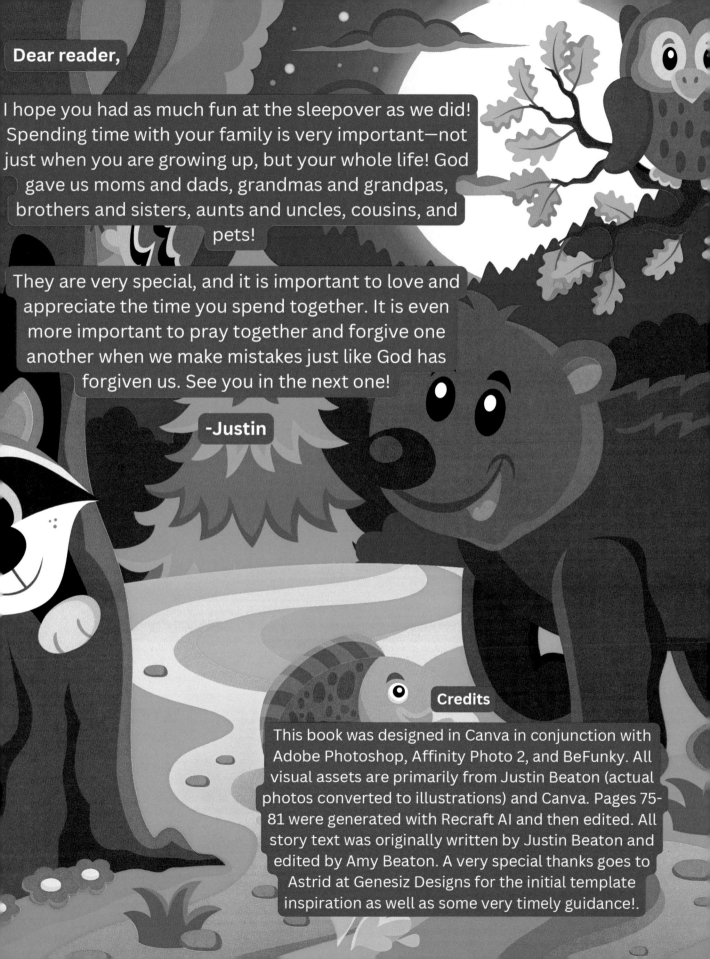

Dear reader,

I hope you had as much fun at the sleepover as we did! Spending time with your family is very important—not just when you are growing up, but your whole life! God gave us moms and dads, grandmas and grandpas, brothers and sisters, aunts and uncles, cousins, and pets!

They are very special, and it is important to love and appreciate the time you spend together. It is even more important to pray together and forgive one another when we make mistakes just like God has forgiven us. See you in the next one!

-Justin

Credits

This book was designed in Canva in conjunction with Adobe Photoshop, Affinity Photo 2, and BeFunky. All visual assets are primarily from Justin Beaton (actual photos converted to illustrations) and Canva. Pages 75-81 were generated with Recraft AI and then edited. All story text was originally written by Justin Beaton and edited by Amy Beaton. A very special thanks goes to Astrid at Genesiz Designs for the initial template inspiration as well as some very timely guidance!.

GOOD
NIGHT